D1278298

NEW YORK STATE'S
Covered Bridges

The bridge at North Blenheim is a fine example of a Long truss, patented by Stephen H. Long in 1830. This postcard of the impressive interior of the Blenheim Bridge shows the large center arch going clear to the ridgepole. The Blenheim Bridge is one of only six double-lane covered bridges still standing in the United States.

POSTCARD HISTORY SERIES

NEW YORK STATE'S
Covered Bridges

Richard R. Wilson

ARCADIA
PUBLISHING

Published by Arcadia Publishing
Charleston, South Carolina

Printed in the United States of America

Library of Congress Catalog Card Number: 2004102493

For all general information contact Arcadia Publishing at:
Telephone 843-853-2070
Fax 843-853-0044
E-mail sales@arcadiapublishing.com
For customer service and orders:
Toll-Free 1-888-313-2665

Visit us on the Internet at www.arcadiapublishing.com

CONTENTS

ACKNOWLEDGMENTS

I want to thank the New York State Covered Bridge Society for allowing me to use the photographs and information included in my column "Card Corner" for the *Empire State Courier*. I also want to thank my wife, Jeanette, for the support over the years in pursuing my covered bridge hobby.

INTRODUCTION

People are surprised to learn that New York State had more than 250 covered bridges at one time. In the early 1800s, bridges were built across New York's many streams and rivers. Our land was mostly forest at that time, so it was only natural to use the timber to make bridges.

But why a covered bridge? Very soon the bridge builders found that if the large timbers were left exposed to the weather, they would rot and the builders would lose their investment. The builders started adding siding and a roof to the bridge structure, and the covered bridge was born. With proper maintenance, the wooden covered bridges would last well over 100 years.

One of New York's prominent bridge builders was Theodore Burr of Torringford, Connecticut. He traveled to New York in the late 1700s and settled in Oxford, New York, where he built a home in 1809. This home is now the Village Library.

Theodore Burr built bridges across the Chenango River, the Mohawk River, the mighty Hudson, and the Schoharie Creek. His bridge at Esperance across Schoharie Creek was the last of his covered bridges to be destroyed. The bridge was removed in 1930. In 1808, Burr built a wooden suspension bridge across the Mohawk River in Schenectady. This 900-foot-long bridge was covered in the 1820s and was removed in 1874.

Burr's masterpiece here in New York was the 800-foot-long bridge that he built across the Hudson River between Waterford and Lansingburgh in 1804. He patented the truss used in this bridge, and today it is known as a Burr truss. This great bridge, which was covered in 1814, lasted for more than 100 years and was destroyed by fire on July 10, 1909.

The only Burr bridge still standing after 1909 was the Esperance Bridge across the Schoharie Creek in Esperance. Burr built this three-span bridge in 1812 with arches that were below the roadway. When it was destroyed in 1930, the reign of Burr-built bridges ended.

The bridges of New York are well represented with the different truss types. Of the 24 old covered bridges still standing, we can see the king post, queen post, Burr, Town, Long, and Howe trusses.

The most outstanding and unique covered bridge still standing in New York State is the Blenheim Bridge over Schoharie Creek at North Blenheim. The great bridge was built in 1855 by Nicholas Montgomery Powers. This bridge, at 210 feet in a clear span, is the longest single-span covered bridge in the world. It is one of only six two-lane covered bridges still in existence in the United States.

The highest concentration of covered bridges in New York State is a three-county area in the Catskills. In Delaware, Sullivan, and Ulster Counties, 16 exist. Northeast of Albany in Washington County, four more covered bridges can be seen, including one that has been converted into a covered bridge museum at Shushan.

Fortunately, the postcard makers of the early years took photographs of covered bridges. These snapshots have now become historic postcards, as the images show bridges now long gone. Real-photo postcards are most desirable because the quality of the image is better than a printed card and because they are extremely rare. Many times, the same negative would be used for printed cards. The printed card could be mass-produced and distributed to more outlets. The printed card could also be enhanced, allowing trees and telephone poles, signs, and other unwanted items to be removed from the image.

Most all covered bridges still in existence in New York State have been depicted on old postcards. When I show a covered bridge that is still standing, I will identify it as one you can still go and see. The chapters are laid out alphabetically, and some counties with few bridges are grouped together. This work shows only part of my postcard collection. New cards and photographs of long-gone covered bridges are continually added to my collection. Please send any information and corrections to Richard Wilson, 6342 Martin Drive, Rome, New York, 13440.

One

ALBANY COUNTY TO DUTCHESS COUNTY

French's Mills—or French's Hollow—Bridge was the last full-size covered bridge in Albany County. Spanning the Normanskill near Guilderland Center, it was built in 1869 by Henry Witherwax and was removed in the summer of 1933. This card is postmarked 1905.

The French's Hollow Bridge was built with a rare truss called the Haupt. Herman Haupt, a railway engineer, devised and patented his truss between 1839 and 1840. The Haupt truss is seen here in the French's Hollow Bridge.

The French's Hollow Bridge was a single-span bridge measuring 162 feet long.

The Waldenville Covered Bridge in Albany County was built by Gen. Hiram Walden in 1830, across the Foxenkill.

Standing in Delevan in Cattaraugus County, this covered bridge was built in 1872 across the Elton Branch of Cattaraugus Creek. The sign on the bridge proclaimed, "Notice: Automobiles Must Slow Down to 4 Miles Per Hour Under Penalty."

The Delevan Bridge, dismantled in 1920 when State Route 16 was built, appears here in a side view. This card is postmarked 1907.

In order to span the Susquehanna River, bridges had to be quite long. At 450 feet long, the bridge at Bainbridge, Chenango County, stretched across the river with four spans. The two-lane bridge was built in 1853 by the Bainbridge Bridge Company. Flood waters damaged the bridge in 1899, and it was removed in the same year.

This old bridge in Norwich was also in Chenango County. Employing the Burr truss, it crossed the Chenango River on East Main Street with two spans and was 170 feet long. The bridge was built in 1845 and was removed in 1892.

The Ryders Mills Bridge in Columbia County was a handsome bridge with open sides showing off the Howe truss. The 113-foot-long, single-span bridge crossed Kinderhook Creek. The white bridge was built in 1870 and was destroyed by a flood on July 22, 1945.

This covered bridge is located in Chatham Center in Columbia County. The old span was built over the Kinderhook Creek in 1870 with a Howe truss.

In Columbia County at Hudson, the Bunker Bridge stood. It was a short Town lattice covered bridge across Claverack Creek, between the towns of Greenport and Claverack on what is now Route 66.

This card shows the Bunker Bridge through the tollgate. A sign on the bridge reads, "All persons are forbidden driving over this bridge faster than a walk. $10.00 fine."

Hudson, N.Y., The Old Bunker Bridge.

This side view of the Bunker Bridge shows that it was not in very good shape in the area of the lower chord.

Columbia County did not have many covered bridges but had a few rare ones, like these twin bridges at Kinderhook. Today, it is hard to find twin covered bridges. This pair was built over the Kinderhook Creek, just south of the village of Kinderhook, in 1840.

This view of "the Kinderhook Twins" shows the two lanes and the dividing wall between them. The bridges were built with a Town truss, and the center part just divided the lanes.

This card shows the Town truss and the open sides that made these bridges so handsome. The bridges were removed in 1920.

About three miles from the Kinderhook Twins was another set of twin covered bridges at Valatie. These two bridges connected Island No. 10 in the Kinderhook to each side of the river. They were also built with a Town truss and had a divided roadway. Constructed in 1840, the Valatie covered bridges were then removed in 1928.

In the village of Cincinnatus in Cortland County stood this covered bridge across the Otselic River. The two-span bridge of 150 feet was built in 1865 and was removed in 1903.

This is the covered bridge at Pleasant Valley in Duchess County. This Town lattice bridge was built in 1845 and was replaced by a modern steel-and-concrete bridge in 1911. Notice the mill dam and the old mill next to the bridge.

Two

DELAWARE COUNTY

OLD WOODEN BRIDGE OVER DELAWARE RIVER AT DEPOSIT, N. Y.

The Deposit Covered Bridge was a 300-foot-long, two-span bridge crossing the West Branch of the Delaware River.

The Deposit Bridge was built by James Lovelace in 1875. He used the Town truss and an arch, which can be seen in this postcard sent in 1912.

The Deposit Covered Bridge was located on present Route 17 and crossed the West Branch of the Delaware River. Note the positive camber in this side view of the bridge.

Seen here is the Deposit Covered Bridge not long before it was replaced in 1928. Route 17 signs are affixed to the portal.

This old covered bridge was built *c.* 1845 by William Richardson at Davenport Center. The 130-foot-long, two-span bridge crossed Charlotte Creek. The span was abandoned in 1935 and was removed five years later.

Fitch's Bridge is located two miles east of Delhi, just off Route 10. This bridge was originally built by James Frazier and James Warren for $1,900 in the village of Delhi. They built a variation of the Town truss in which the first plank is near vertical, the second inclines more, and by about the fourth one, the normal angle is reached.

In 1885, a new iron bridge replaced the covered bridge. David Wright and a town crew dismantled and moved the covered bridge three miles up the West Branch of the Delaware River to a place called Fitch's Crossing. The timbers and planks were marked in black paint, and these markings can still be seen today.

When this 100-foot-long Town lattice bridge was re-erected, it was installed in the opposite direction from the way it stood in Delhi. The beams marked "east" are on the west side, and those marked "west" are on the east side. Fitch's Bridge underwent a complete reconstruction in 2001, and some of the historical radiating Town truss was destroyed. Its new appearance looks nothing like these old postcards.

(Mot) By a Dam Site, Hamden, N. Y.

The Hamden Covered Bridge still stands and can be seen just off Route 10 at the north end of the village of Hamden. Robert Murray built this 128-foot-long span in 1859 across the West Branch of the Delaware River. The bridge was restored from 2000 to 2001.

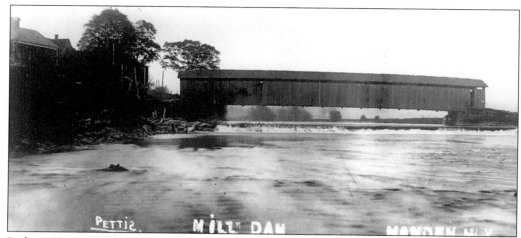

Robert Murray built this bridge with the now rare Long truss, which was patented by Col. Stephen H. Long in 1830. The cost to build the Hamden Covered Bridge in 1859 was $1,000. It can still be seen off Route 10 in Hamden.

The Colchester Bridge was a 318-foot-long, two-span bridge located two miles south of Downsville. Robert Murray built the bridge in 1834 across the East Branch of the Delaware River. It was closed to traffic in July 1947. One span fell into the river on January 1, 1948, and six months later the bridge was gone.

Not much is known about the Sidney Covered Bridge. Using a Burr truss, it crossed the Susquehanna River on Bridge Street. It was built in 1852 and was replaced by an iron bridge in 1894.

The Wattles' Ferry Bridge crossed the Susquehanna River at Unadilla. The bridge was built by Bissell and Sluman Wattles in 1817. It stretched 250 feet in three spans. The old bridge was removed in 1894.

The right of way for over $^3/_4$ of a Century.
Over the Delaware River at Downsville, N. Y.

The Downsville Covered Bridge is a 174-foot-long, single-span Long truss with an auxiliary queen post. Robert Murray constructed the bridge for $1,700 in 1854. This bridge can still be seen in the village of Downsville.

View of the Delaware River showing the Old Covered Bridge, Downsville, N. Y.

The Downsville Bridge is the second oldest covered bridge still in use in New York State.

The Downsville Bridge spans the East Branch of the Delaware River just downstream from the Downsville Dam, which holds back the waters of the Pepacton Reservoir.

Lower part of Downsville--Big Flood in Delaware, April 9, 1895.

This view of Downsville shows how well Robert Murray built the covered bridge. Before the Downsville Dam was built in the 1950s, the Delaware River flooded often. In this photograph of the flood of 1895, the bridge stands high and dry while the water goes around it.

The Right-of-Way Over the Delaware for a Century, Downsville, N. Y.

The Downsville Bridge's Pony truss is visible on the village side. This card was postmarked in Downsville in 1916.

The Rockland Bridge spanned Spring Brook near the Beaverkill at Rockland. The 125-foot-long Town lattice truss was constructed by a Mr. Davidson in 1830. This bridge could have been preserved, but instead it was removed in 1948 and replaced by a steel bridge.

The Trout Creek Bridge was built by George Lovelace in 1850 near Cannonsville. This postcard shows the bridge before the roof was raised in 1923.

This view of the Trout Creek Bridge shows it with its raised roof. The old bridge was replaced with a new one in 1948, and it was moved into the field next to the bridge. Later, the structure was moved to Sidney to be part of an old village, but vandals set it on fire. Half of the bridge burned. The part that remained was transported to New Milford, Pennsylvania, where it was cut in two to form a smaller covered bridge for an old village.

The Covered Bridge, Dunraven, N. Y.

This bridge was built near Dunraven and crossed the Platte Kill, or Flat Brook as it was called at times. This short 38-foot-long bridge was built by William Mead in 1870. It appears to have been a multiple king-post truss. In 1935, the bridge was moved to Arena and placed over the Mill Brook on property owned by the Tuscarora Club. In recent years, the bridge has become less accessible to the public, as the club will not give permission to visit the site.

The Arkville Covered Bridge, a 90-foot-long Town lattice truss, was built in 1848 across the Dry Brook. This old card includes an advertising sign for "Tom Platt 5¢ cigars."

The Old Covered Bridge, Arkville, N. Y.

The Arkville Bridge crossed the Dry Brook about one-half mile above the confluence with the Delaware River. It is located on today's Route 28 at the point where the Dry Brook Road intersects Route 28.

Old Covered Bridge. ARKVILLE, Catskill Mountains, N. Y.

The Arkville Bridge was replaced in 1938 by a steel-and-concrete bridge. It was the last covered bridge on any state road in New York.

OLD COVERED BRIDGE, NEAR MARGARETVILLE, N.Y.

Dunraven N.Y.

The Dunraven Station Covered Bridge was built by William Mead across the East Branch of the Delaware River in 1870. The Town truss was used, but it also had two large king-post trusses on each side. It was originally a 136-foot-long, single-span bridge, but in later years a center pier, made from wood piling, was added.

Old Covered Bridge, Crossing the Delaware River near Margaretville Catskill Mountains, N. Y.

The Dunraven Station Bridge, also known as the Stone Schoolhouse Bridge, should still be standing. The bridge was torn down in 1956 because of the construction of the Pepacton Reservoir. Since the waters of the reservoir have never reached its location, one can walk down the dirt road off old Route 28 to where the bridge once stood. If one could cross the river, the road would go past the railroad station and up past the Stone Schoolhouse, which still stands as a historic landmark.

The Halcottsville Covered Bridge was built in 1870 by brothers William and John Utter. They constructed a 75-foot-long, single-span Town truss across the East Branch of the Delaware River.

Just upstream from the Halcottsville Covered Bridge was a stone dam that created Lake Wawaka. The lake produced the waterpower needed to run the gristmill located beside the covered bridge. The mill was so close to the bridge that part of the entrance for the mill was at the portal of the bridge.

In 1864, James William Coulter built a Town lattice covered bridge across the Beaverkill at Cooks Falls. One abutment was built on a natural rock ledge, while the other was built of dry-laid stone.

Cooks Falls was situated on both sides of the Beaverkill; the bridge was a passage from Route 17 to the business section. A nice, arched iron span was an approach to one end of the bridge.

This card of Cooks Falls shows the portal and some advertising pasted to the bridge. Typical of Catskill covered bridges, it incorporated buttresses and a radiating Town truss.

In the early 1930s, three drunken men were charged with blowing up the Cooks Falls Bridge. The bridge was not destroyed but was badly damaged. After being repaired by Sherman Francisco, it continued in service until it was removed in 1948.

DeLancey is located about one mile upstream from the Hamden Covered Bridge. Robert Murray erected the DeLancey Bridge in 1859 across the West Branch of the Delaware River.

Delancey, N. Y.

The 118-foot-long DeLancey span was constructed using a Long truss. John and Charley Cobb, who lived in DeLancey, cut and delivered the wood used in the bridge's construction for $7 per thousand board feet. The bridge burned in a suspicious fire on August 14, 1940.

OLD COVERED BRIDGE NEAR UNADILLA, N.Y.

This old bridge was about two miles from Unadilla on Covered Bridge Road and one mile from where the Ouleout empties into the Susquehanna River. This neat 96-foot-long bridge was built in 1874 by Slolmon Youmans, a farmer and carpenter.

25—Old Covered Bridge, Unadilla, N. Y.

The Unadilla Bridge was built with a very unusual truss. The main truss was a queen post, which held two other queen-post trusses within it. The bridge was removed the week of May 25, 1956.

In 1865, Robert Murray built a covered bridge in Margaretville across the East Branch of the Delaware River. He had built bridges at other locations using the Long patent truss, but in the 100-foot-long Margaretville span, he used the Town truss.

The railroad ran very near the portal of the Margaretville Bridge. Large openings on both sides made the bridge very distinctive. The portal advertising reads, "4 Up To Date Clothing, Ladies, Gents & Childrens Furnishings, Cullen & Shutz."

to the gum working as hard as ever? Carrie

2846 The old covered bridge, Margaretville N.Y.

This old view of the Margaretville Bridge shows just how close the railroad came to the covered bridge. A sign on the portal reads, "Five Dollars Fine For Riding Or Driving Over This Bridge Faster Than A Walk." The bridge was replaced in 1932.

The Sexsmith Covered Bridge near Davenport appears in this postcard. The bridge was built between 1836 and 1837 across Middle Brook Stream, which flows into Charlotte Creek. The bridge was on present Route 23, and in 1915, a new road was built that bypassed the bridge. The bridge was removed in 1916.

River Bridge, Hawleys, N. Y.

B 3142

The Hawleys Bridge was located just downstream from the Hamden Bridge. The 128-foot-long bridge was built in 1859 by Robert Murray for $600. The Long truss bridge crossed the West Branch of the Delaware River. After being torn down in 1948, it was replaced by an iron bridge.

OLD COVERED BRIDGE AT ARENA N. Y.   B 27 C   NYSPIX COMMERCE

The Halls Bridge spanned the East Branch of the Delaware near Dunraven and just over two miles above Arena. The 108-foot-long windowed bridge was laid out by William Mead and was built by Nelson Thompson in 1869. Flood waters destroyed the bridge as it was being removed in 1955. The site is now underwater.

When viewing photographs of the Pepacton Bridge, one first notices the large buttresses. The Pepacton Bridge, built in 1857 by Robert Murray, was a 168-foot-long span across the East Branch of the Delaware River.

The most unusual aspect of the Pepacton Bridge is that Robert Murray used the rare Haupt truss when building it. He also used the radiating truss at the beginning. The bridge was doomed, as it would be enveloped by the waters of the Pepacton Reservoir; however, before it could be removed, it was taken out by floodwaters and wind on November 25, 1950.

The Colchester Station Bridge, or Weed's Bridge as it was also sometimes called, was built by Robert Murray in 1870 across the West Branch of the Delaware River near Walton. The 138-foot-long Town truss also incorporated the radiating truss and an arch. The bridge was closed in April 1950 and was burned by the highway department on February 14, 1951.

The Horton Covered Bridge was a 200-foot-long Town truss across the Beaverkill. It was replaced in 1934 by a steel bridge taken from the village of East Branch.

Three

ESSEX COUNTY TO HAMILTON COUNTY

The Jay Covered Bridge, located in the village of Jay in Essex County, was built across the East Branch of the Ausable River by George M. Burt in 1857 with a Howe truss. This card shows the single 175-foot-long Howe truss span.

This postcard of the Jay Bridge shows the two smaller spans. One is a Stringer, and the other is a queen-post truss. The total length of the bridge was 240 feet until 1954, when the two small spans were removed, leaving only the 175-foot-long bridge.

This view looks up the Ausable River to the dam above the rocks. At the time of this writing, the Jay Bridge, after sitting on land for a few years, was being dismantled to be restored and put back over the river in 2005 or 2006.

River or bridge at Boquet.

Boquet is located in Essex County, just off Route 22. This single-span covered bridge crossed the Boquet River. This card was postmarked in Boquet on August 22, 1910.

The Wales Center Bridge was located in Erie County and crossed Buffalo Creek on present Route 20A. This Town lattice covered bridge was replaced in 1927.

The Bullis Hill Bridge was situated in Erie County across Big Buffalo Creek, between Elma and Marilla. The bridge was built in 1859 and was removed in 1926.

This is another view of the Bullis Hill Bridge. The Town truss was reinforced with a queen-post truss.

South Bombay, in Franklin County, held this nice Town lattice covered bridge over the Little Salmon River. The bridge was built in 1876 and was replaced in 1947.

Franklin County was also home to this long three-span bridge across the St. Regis River. Built in 1862, the bridge at Hogansburg was replaced in 1931.

The Silkworth Lantry Toy Factory, Hogansburg, N. Y.

In this image of the Hogansburg Bridge across the large St. Regis River, note the old mills along the river.

BRIDGE AT FISH HOUSE N.Y. 62.

The Fish House Bridge was located in Fulton County near Northampton. This two-lane covered bridge crossed the Sacandaga River with a 400-foot-long, three-span Burr arch.

The Fish House Bridge was built in 1818 by Daniel Stewart and friendly American Indians for a cost of $5,500. Timbers came from virgin forests in the Fish House area and were hewn at the bridge site. Trees for the lower chords of the bridge were reported to have reached 96 feet in length.

The Fish House Bridge had an unusual portal. It was very much like a porch with its own roof.

The Fish House Bridge was still in place when the waters of the Sacandaga Reservoir rose in 1930. Villagers were going to try and save it, but on April 23, 1930, heavy winds and big waves damaged the bridge. Some of the timbers were recovered and later used in building garages in the area.

Bridge across Sacandago River at Osborn Bridge, N.Y.

Another bridge across the Sacandaga in Fulton County was the long two-span Osborn Bridge.

The Osborn Bridge was burned in 1929 to make way for the new reservoir.

This covered bridge was in Ephratah, Fulton County, and crossed Caroga Creek not far from the Saltsman Hotel. This card is postmarked, "Ephratah, N.Y., August 5, 1911."

Cauterskill Bridge, Catskill Mountains, N. Y. *10-14-07 — Got here O.K. this evening. Sorry I can not join you. Go to the Mountains tomorrow. Bill.*

Few covered bridges were built in Greene County. Seen here, the Cauterskill Bridge, near Catskill, crossed Kaaterskill Creek. This card is postmarked 1907.

CATSKILL, N.Y. OLD COVERED BRIDGE.   D. D. Horton, Souvenirs.

The Cauterskill Bridge was located just above where the water tumbled over the rocks making nice falls. Upstream was calm, and the bridge's reflection was visible in the still water.

This is the only Hamilton County bridge covered in this book. This bridge was built over Sacandaga River just north of the village of Wells.

OLD COVERED BRIDGE, BUILT 1866, WELLS, N.Y. ADIRONDACK MOUNTAINS.

The Wells Covered Bridge was a long two-span Town lattice bridge built in 1866.

The portal of the Wells Covered Bridge is seen here. The photograph looks like it was taken from an old car, as part of the post for the windshield can be seen.

Pictured here is the Wells Covered Bridge after a dam was built downstream, resulting in Lake Algonquin. The waters rose to near the bottom of the covered bridge, but the bridge survived until it was replaced by a new one in 1932.

Four

Herkimer County to Oneida County

North of Herkimer in Herkimer County stood the Dempster's Bridge, a three-span structure across the West Canada Creek. The railroad crossed the road near the portal, which resulted in a train and car accident on May 14, 1911. Four people were killed. The bridge was replaced by a concrete arch structure in 1921.

Old Brockett's Bridge, removed in 1903

Dolgeville was at one time known as Brockett's Bridge. The covered bridge by that name was a two-span structure across the East Canada Creek on what is now Route 29. The bridge was replaced in 1893.

This is a portal view of Brockett's Bridge in Dolgeville. The two-span bridge was built with a multiple king-post truss with an arch. The bridge crossed the East Canada Creek between Herkimer and Fulton Counties.

Just north of Dolgeville on Hopson Road was this covered bridge built by Alvah Hopson, noted bridge builder, in the town of Salisbury. The bridge was replaced in 1926 by a concrete structure, which is still in place over Spruce Creek in Herkimer County.

McDOUGAL FALLS, SALISBURY CENTER, N. Y.

Salisbury Center is located in Herkimer County just north of Dolgeville. The Salisbury Center Covered Bridge still stands across Spruce Creek in the center of the village. The bridge is situated just above McDougal Falls, which is spectacular in spring.

Old Covered Bridge
Town of Salisbury

HADCOCK'S SNACK BAR - SALISBURY, NEW YORK

The Salisbury Center Bridge was built in 1875 by Alvah Hopson, the man who is credited with building six covered bridges in the town of Salisbury.

The 50-foot-long Salisbury Center Covered Bridge was built with a multiple king-post truss and an arch. This postcard was the first color chrome card published of the bridge. Richard Wilson took the photograph in 1967, with his wife and three girls on the open bridge. This card is postmarked April 1969.

Another covered bridge in Salisbury Center was located just south of the village across Spruce Creek. It was known as Moore's Mill Bridge and was on present State Route 29. One of the old signs reads, "Boats, Shoes, and Rubbers, Hats, Caps, at Weavers, Dolgeville, N.Y."

Salisbury Ctr., N.Y.

If one travels through the existing Salisbury Center Bridge and turns left onto Kingsley Street, one will cross a concrete bridge spanning Spruce Creek. The present bridge replaced this covered bridge built by Alvah Hopson.

This postcard shows the Kingsley Bridge above Elwell Falls in Spruce Creek. If this bridge had not been replaced, both the Salisbury Center Bridge and this one could be seen at the same time.

This covered bridge near Poland crossed the West Canada Creek between the counties of Oneida and Herkimer. This single-span structure was called the Schermerhorn Bridge.

AUTO CAMPING GROUNDS AND OLD COVERED BRIDGE IN THE KUYAHOORA VALLEY, POLAND, N. Y

This postcard of the Schermerhorn Bridge shows an early rest area or auto park near the bridge. This interesting hand-painted card was made in France.

Covered Bridge near Poland, N.Y.   Aug 29 - 1926

The Schermerhorn Bridge is seen here in its final days. Notice that this covered bridge also had a short iron bridge on one end. This postcard is dated August 29, 1926, and the covered bridge was replaced by an iron bridge in 1927.

East Creek, N.Y. Old Toll Gate.

Between Herkimer and Montgomery Counties, this long three-span toll bridge could be found crossing East Canada Creek. This card shows the tollhouse and the covered bridge through the gate.

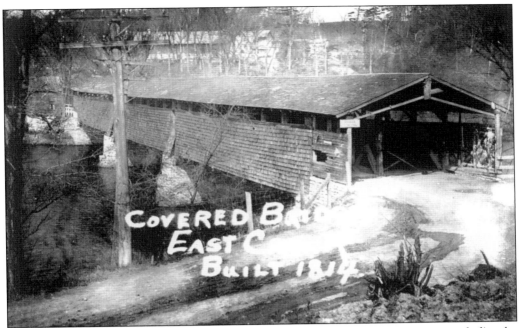

The East Creek Bridge is reported to have been built in 1812, but some postcards list the construction date as 1814. The bridge was located on what is now Route 5 near the Beardslee Castle. A crumbling concrete arch bridge is at this location today.

The East Creek Bridge was a three-span, two-lane bridge with shingled siding. This photograph was taken in February 1911 of Dr. C. C. Vedder and F. S. Mosher. The covered bridge was removed in 1912 and was replaced by the concrete arch bridge.

COVERED BRIDGE 1814-1910 EAST CREEK N.Y.   PHOTO BY SPICER'S

This side view shows almost the full length of this three-span, two-lane East Creek Bridge. The investors who owned this bridge got their money's worth, as it lasted for 100 years.

MONITOR MILLS
ELLISBURG N.Y.

This small covered bridge was located at Monitor Mills at Ellisburg in Jefferson County. This 62-foot-long Burr truss bridge was built in 1866 over Sandy Creek. It was removed in 1910.

At Allendale in Jefferson County, this single-span Town lattice bridge crossed the south branch of Sandy Creek. The date on the back of this postcard is June 17, 1910. The message reads, "This bridge has been standing 50 years, is soon to be torn down." Indeed it *was* replaced in 1910.

The Upper Bridge at Ellisburg in Jefferson County crossed Big Sandy Creek. This Burr truss bridge was located just downstream from a dam and a mill and was removed in 1913. This postcard dates from July 1908.

This postcard, mailed in 1910, bears the photograph of the Log London Bridge in Pierrepont Manor. The Burr truss bridge spanned the south branch of Sandy Creek. The message on the card reads, "This is the old bridge just torn down to be replaced by an iron one. Partly on our farm."

This long view of Dexter, Jefferson County, shows the covered bridge across the Black River. This three-span bridge was built in 1848 and was replaced in 1900.

Five

LIVINGSTON COUNTY TO PUTNAM COUNTY

In 1830, Russell Daboll of Mount Morris built a two-lane Town lattice covered bridge over the Genesee River at Geneseo in Livingston County. The bridge was replaced in 1913 by an open steel span.

The Geneseo Bridge bore interesting wooden abutments. Built of timbers, they were braced inside and covered with plank on the outside. On either end of the bridge were wooden approaches, which had to be replaced many times.

This covered bridge was located in Mount Morris in Livingston County. The two-span bridge crossed the Genesee River.

This card shows part of the railroad covered bridge over falls in Honeoye Falls, Monroe County. The bridge was built in 1853 and was replaced by an iron bridge in 1893. In the foreground is a rare Whipple iron bowstring arch bridge.

Amsterdam, in Montgomery County, had a covered bridge across the Mohawk River. The bridge was built in 1843 as a three-span, but one span washed away in 1865 and was replaced by an iron bridge.

Jacks Reef Covered Bridge was located in Onondaga County, only 15 miles west of Syracuse. The bridge was erected across the Seneca River by Aaron Vedder. He used the Town truss to construct three spans of 98 feet each, with a total length of 305 feet.

Boating was popular at the Jacks Reef Bridge. Postmarked "Jordan, N.Y. May 28, 1914," this card shows the boat docks and two spans of the bridge.

This postcard of the Jacks Reef Bridge depicts the two lanes and the long bridge. The bridge was divided in the center, making two roadways with a width of 11 feet each. It was sided only halfway, so this long bridge was not a dark tunnel.

Old Covered Bridge over Mohawk River, Canajoharie, N.Y.

This old bridge across the Mohawk River was at Canajoharie in Montgomery County. This two-lane arch bridge also crossed the railroad tracks on the north side. It was destroyed by fire in 1901.

Brooks Bridge
Blooming Grove,
N. Y.

The Brooks Bridge was in the town of Blooming Grove near Washingtonville in Orange County. Brooks Bridge crossed Moodna Creek with a span of 80 feet. The sign on the right side of the portal is for an auction on October 15, 1907.

This side view of Brooks Bridge shows the horizontal siding and the arches of the Burr truss ending in an abutment. This card is postmarked 1909.

The Brooks Bridge in Washingtonville used a six-panel Burr truss. The bridge was built in 1840 and was removed in 1922, when the highway department straightened the road.

22—Old Covered Bridge, Richfield Springs, N. Y.

This small covered bridge just south of Richfield Springs in Otsego County was built in 1830 on what is now Route 28.

The Richfield Springs Covered Bridge stood just above a dam in Mink Creek. The bridge had horizontal siding and scallops all along the roofline.

This view of the Richfield Springs Covered Bridge shows the pond created by the dam and the scallops on the roofline of the portal. The barn seen through the bridge has these same scallops along the roofline. The bridge was replaced in 1935.

The River Bridge in Otego, Otsego County, crossed the Susquehanna River. This long two-span covered bridge was built by Robert Murray in 1866 and was replaced by an iron bridge in 1901. This card is postmarked 1909.

Oneonta had a covered bridge that crossed the Susquehanna River on Main Street in two spans. William Richardson built the bridge in 1835 for $1,000. It was replaced in 1888.

The old Colliers Covered Bridge was a landmark that stood near Oneonta in Otsego County for nearly 100 years. It was built in 1832 across the Susquehanna on today's Route 7.

The Colliers Bridge was built by Capt. Edward Thorn. He used 3-by-10-inch Native Hemlock timbers to fashion the Town lattice truss. The bridge was in constant use for 97 years and was finally removed in 1929.

This covered bridge in Carlton in Orleans County was called "the Two Bridges." It was built in 1848 across Oak Orchard Creek and was removed in 1910.

This postcard captures the rare railroad covered bridge, this one located in Towners, Putnam County. The bridge was a single-span, single-track Howe truss built in 1881.

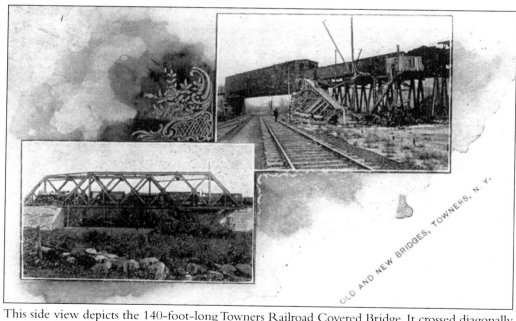

This side view depicts the 140-foot-long Towners Railroad Covered Bridge. It crossed diagonally over tracks of the New York and Harlem Railroad. It was replaced in 1906 by the New York, New Haven, and Harlem Railroad. The message on the back reads, "Waiting here for train." The card is postmarked October 12, 1909.

Six

SULLIVAN, ULSTER, AND WYOMING COUNTIES

The Halls Mills Covered Bridge in Sullivan County near Claryville is a covered bridge that still stands today. Built in 1912 by David Benton and John Knight over the Neversink River, the single-span Town truss bridge spans 130 feet. The bridge was bypassed in the early 1960s, and it now stands just downstream from the new Hunter Road Bridge. This postcard was sent from Claryville in 1918.

The Beaverkill Bridge in Sullivan County is another covered bridge one can still visit. John Davidson built this 98-foot-long Town lattice bridge across the Beaverkill in 1865. Follow signs to the Beaverkill State Park and the bridge will be visible. This card is postmarked 1908.

This postcard of the Beaverkill Bridge shows the nice dry-laid stones used in the abutments. The Civilian Conservation Corps (CCC) also did much work to build the state park in the 1930s. A sign by the bridge is dedicated to the CCC, 1932–1942.

The Neversink Bridge, a long Town truss, was in Sullivan County just off Route 55, about six miles south of the Halls Mills Covered Bridge. This site is now underwater.

The Neversink Bridge always had an open king-post or queen-post span at each end. The bridge looks very much like those built by John Davidson.

In 1860, John Davidson built a 100-foot-long Town lattice covered bridge in Livingston Manor, Sullivan County. This bridge took Main Street across the Willowemoc Creek. Connected to one end of the covered bridge was a small open king-post span.

In 1913, Livingston Manor replaced the covered bridge. Half of the span was moved up the Willowemoc Creek and re-erected near Debruce, where it is now known as the Bendo Bridge. It is one of the covered bridges in New York State that is still in use.

Woodbourne is located in Sullivan County on Route 52 between Liberty and Ellenville. This bridge crossed the Neversink River with a two-span Burr truss. The card tells us that the bridge was erected in 1844 and was replaced by an iron bridge in 1903.

This card of the Woodbourne Bridge shows one span of the two. The entrance to the bridge is very close to one of the buildings.

The Parkson Bridge was located on the road between Livingston Manor and Debruce in Sullivan County. It employed a Town lattice truss across the Willowemoc Creek.

Mongaup Valley is located on Route 17B about seven miles west of Monticello in Sullivan County. The covered bridge was built in 1830 on the old Newburg-Colchester Turnpike.

1702 COVERE BRIDGE, MONGAUP VALLEY, SULLIVAN CO., N.Y.

This side view of the Mongaup Valley Covered Bridge shows its two spans. Abandonment of this last turnpike road in the state of New York took place in the fall of 1910, and the bridge was replaced on December 5, 1910.

The Bridgeville Covered Bridge in Sullivan County has the honor of being the first covered bridge built in New York State. Bridgeville is located about four miles east of Monticello on Route 17. This old bridge was built across the Neversink River by Maj. Salmon Wheat in 1807.

BURNS & TAYLOR CLOTHIERS.

DRY GOODS
Burns &
Taylors

Burns & Taylors
IS THE PLACE
TO GET YOUR MONEY'S
WORTH

covered bridge at Bridgeville, N. Y., 1807 Centennial 1907

Pub. by Burns & Taylor. (German

This postcard of the Bridgeville Covered Bridge shows how unusual this two-lane bridge was. Note the sidewalk that goes through the center of the bridge. Burns & Taylor was a store in Monticello, only four miles away.

The Bridgeville Covered Bridge was a 160-foot-long, single-span clapboard structure with windows to let some light into the dark tunnel.

This additional view shows the portal on the other end of the Bridgeville Covered Bridge. Major Wheat built well because his masterpiece had lasted more than 100 years—from 1807 to 1923, when it was demolished after a new iron bridge was constructed alongside it.

This old card shows the Van Tran Flat Covered Bridge in Livingston Manor. This Sullivan County span was built across the Willowemoc Creek by John Davidson in 1860.

The Van Tran Flat Bridge in Livingston Manor stood high on dry-laid stone abutments. To get to the south end, one had to drive up a ramp. This bridge still stands and can be seen from the new Route 17.

This side view of the Livingston Manor Bridge looks down the Willowemoc Creek. The bridge was repaired in 1984, when large laminated arches were installed so it could handle heavier traffic.

The Turnwood Covered Bridge appears here in its original location across the Beaverkill in the town of Hardenburg in Ulster County. The bridge was built in 1885 by Nelson Tompkins.

In the 1930s, the Turnwood Bridge was taken apart and moved to its present location near Olive Bridge. It is now known as the Ashoken-Turnwood Bridge. This postcard shows the bridge in its original location.

Perrine's Bridge is located north of New Paltz in Ulster County, just off Route 32 onto Route 213. The 154-foot-long Burr truss bridge was built by Benjamin West in 1844 across the Wallkill. It can be seen from the northbound lane of the New York State Thruway. This old card is postmarked 1907.

This covered bridge was located between the towns of Mount Marion and Ruby in Ulster County. It crossed the Platte Kill on the old King's Highway. This Town truss bridge was destroyed by fire on April 26, 1933.

In Ganahgote, Ulster County, this covered bridge crossed the Shawangunk River. Sometimes known as the Tuttletown Bridge, this span was built in 1845 with a Burr truss and was removed in the 1930s.

The Mill Hook Bridge spanned the Mombaccus Creek at Mill Hook in Ulster County.

"The Forge," near Jay Gould's Summer Residence
Arkville, N. Y. — Catskill Mountains, N. Y.

The Forge Covered Bridge in Ulster County was the shortest covered bridge on New York's highway system. Jerome Moot built this king-post bridge in December 1906 and January 1907. The town of Hardenburg owned the bridge until 1953, when it was bought by Kingdon V. Gould for $1. The bridge crosses the Dry Brook with a 27-foot-long span. Today, the bridge has a gate across the portal so no one can drive through it.

The covered bridge across Rondout Creek in Ulster County was a connecting link between the village of Napanoch and the New York State Reform School near Ellenville. The covered bridge, a 13-panel Burr truss, was replaced in 1935.

This postcard of the Napanoch Bridge shows the New York State Reform School in the background.

Bishop's Falls at Brown's Station was located in Ulster County about 12 miles west of Kingston. The long single-span Town lattice bridge stood high above the Esopus Creek. This entire scene is now under the waters of the Ashoken Reservoir.

This view of the Bishop's Falls Covered Bridge was taken from upstream near the mills and falls. Snow is on the ground, and the very high water is a blur as it rushes toward the bridge. The bridge was gone by 1910.

The old covered Bridge, Wawarsing, N. Y.

The covered bridge at Wawarsing in Ulster County was a long Burr truss across Rondout Creek.

THE OLD COVERED BRIDGE, WALLKILL, N.Y.

In the village of Wallkill, Ulster County, this covered bridge crossed the Wallkill River with a two-span Howe truss. A small iron Pony truss was attached to the village side. The old sign on the bridge reads, "5.00 fine for any person driving over this bridge faster than a walk."

This card shows the side view of the Wallkill Covered Bridge and was postmarked in Wallkill on May 28, 1914.

This little Town lattice covered bridge could be found in Wyoming County, town of Bennington, in Bennington Center. It crossed the north branch of Cayuga Creek on present Route 77 and was washed out in the spring of 1916.

Seven

RENSSELAER COUNTY TO TOMPKINS COUNTY

Shedd's Bridge was located near the Bennington Battle Field in Rensselaer County near the Vermont border. Also known as Burgess Bridge, it was built in 1850, crossing the Walloomsac River with a Town truss. While being repaired in 1947, a jack used to prop it up was stolen. The bridge collapsed on October 1, 1947, and was damaged beyond repair.

The Upper Bridge crossed the Little Hoosic River at the village of Petersburg in Rensselaer County. It was located on today's New York Route 2 and was replaced by a concrete arch bridge in 1911.

The Lower Bridge at the village of Petersburg was also known as the Wells Bridge. Longer than the Upper Bridge, this Town lattice structure spanned the Little Hoosic River near the old mills. In this postcard, the falls can be seen on the other side of the bridge. This bridge was also replaced in 1911 by a concrete arch structure.

The Whitehouse, or Long, Bridge was located on old Route 7 near Hoosic in Rensselaer County. The bridge was built across the Hoosic River by Robert Gardner and his son Charles in 1840.

This view of the Whitehouse Bridge shows the south entrance, where one could take Route 7 across the bridge to Hoosic or Route 22 to the east to Hoosic Falls. This part of Route 7 was relocated in 1933, and the old bridge was removed in October 1933.

The Little Hoosic River Bridge on Route 7 spanned a slough, or backwater, of the Hoosic River. If one traveled on the Whitehouse Bridge, one would immediately cross this bridge on the way to Hoosic. The Whitehouse Bridge is visible through the portal. The Little Hoosic River Bridge was washed out by the 1938 hurricane floods and was dismantled in March 1939.

Perhaps this covered bridge between Waterford and Lansingburgh, crossing the Hudson River, was the greatest covered bridge in New York State. The old bridge was built by the famous builder Theodore Burr in 1804 for $50,000. It was not covered at the time it was built; the roof was added in 1814.

This view of the two-lane, four-span Waterford Bridge shows its great length of 797 feet. The message on this card describes what happened to the bridge: "You will never cross this Waterford Bridge again as it burned down Saturday. There is only a little left standing on this side. It was quite a sight to see how it was burning." The card is postmarked July 14, 1909.

This west-end view of the Waterford Bridge reveals the trolley-car tracks. Tolls in 1814 were 13¢ for a vehicle with two horses, 10¢ for one horse, and 2¢ each for pedestrians.

After more than 100 years of service, the old Waterford Bridge caught fire and burned on July 10, 1909. The bridge was located between Saratoga County and Rensselaer County. This view shows three spans on fire, with one having already collapsed.

In this view, three spans have now collapsed, and smoke and steam rises from the ruins. Many people wanted to get a closeup look at the bridge burning.

102

Shown is the aftermath of the Waterford fire. One span did not burn, and people tried to get a closer look. The trolley-car tracks, draped over the piers, are still visible here.

This is a view of the upstream side of the burned Waterford Bridge. The span that still stands here had windows in the upper part of the bridge near the roof. Part of the burned truss is starting to float downstream. This span was removed, and a new steel bridge was built on the old piers.

This postcard shows the Waterford Bridge and its replacement. This replacement bridge still exists and is in use between Waterford and Lansingburgh.

The Schaghticoke Hill Bridge crossed the Tomhannock Creek in Rensselaer County. Located on what is now Route 40, the Town lattice span was replaced in 1920.

This covered bridge at Glens Falls was built in 1842 across the falls in the Hudson River, between Saratoga County and Warren County. It was removed in 1890. The photographs for this postcard were taken by the famous Adirondack photographer S. R. Stoddard.

Shown here is the bridge at Esperance in Schoharie County. In 1809, a contract for a new bridge at Esperance was given to Theodore Burr. He constructed the piers in that year and then was called away. He returned in 1811, and on January 12, 1812, the bridge was formally opened to traffic.

The Esperance Bridge was a massive three-span structure with two roadways. There were three large arches below the roadway, and the truss was built upon the arches.

This interior of the Esperance Bridge reveals the massive beams making up the truss built on the arch. Notice the level roadway.

This side view of the Esperance Bridge shows the three long arched spans. After 118 years, the last bridge still in existence built by Theodore Burr was gone! The bridge was replaced in 1930.

The Barnerville Bridge was located between Cobleskill and Howe Cave and crossed the Cobleskill Creek. It was replaced between 1920 and 1922. This card was sent from Howe Cave on February 5, 1911.

Covered Bridge, Howe's Cave, N. Y.

The Howe's Cave Bridge was constructed over the Cobleskill Creek at the junction of Route 7 and the road leading to Howe Cave. The Town truss bridge was removed in 1921.

The Blenheim Covered Bridge is perhaps New York State's most famous covered bridge. Located on Route 30 in the village of North Blenheim in Schoharie County, it is the longest single-span covered bridge in the world and is one of only six covered bridges in the United States with two lanes. This view shows the bridge when it was still in use.

Longest Single Span Wood Bridge in the World, Blenhiem, N.Y.
Postmarked Aug 17, 1909

The Blenheim Covered Bridge was built across the Schoharie Creek by Nicholas M. Powers between 1854 and 1855. It was constructed on the flats in back of the village, then taken apart and erected on scaffolding in the river. Some people called it "Powers's Folley" and said the bridge would not even hold its own weight.

The Longest Single Span Wooden Bridge In The World—231 Ft. Long, Situated At Blenheim, New York.

Powers climbed on the roof of the Blenheim Covered Bridge and remarked, "If the bridge goes down, I never want to see the sun rise again!" He ordered his men to knock out the supports, and the bridge settled about one-quarter inch. It still stands today. This card is postmarked June 26, 1907.

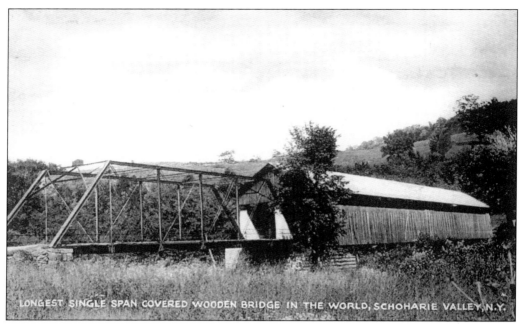

The Blenheim Covered Bridge was 210 feet long in a clear span between the abutments. The total length of the bridge was 228 feet long. In 1869, a freshet washed out a channel across the western approach. A wooden extension was erected, which lasted until 1887, when this iron span was built. The old covered bridge was retired in 1932.

The covered bridge in the upper village of North Blenheim was built over the West Kill by William H. Lloyd in 1884. The five-panel arch truss was removed in 1926.

The Warner Bridge in Schoharie County spanned the West Creek. The bridge, located at Warnerville between Cobleskill and Richmondville, was removed in 1930.

Barners Bridge, located at Cobleskill in Schoharie County, was built across the Cobleskill Creek by Mr. Westfall in 1869.

An old sign on Barners Bridge proclaimed, "Penalty $15.00 for riding or driving faster than a walk over this bridge." The Town truss structure was built for $2,250.

South Grand Street and Boat House, Cobleskill, N. Y.   13414

Barners Bridge was located on Grand Street next to the fairgrounds. This view shows the boathouse, now a part of the fairgrounds.

This long, snakelike structure built in Schenectady across the Mohawk River was constructed by Theodore Burr between 1808 and 1809. He tried an experimental structure in wood—a wooden suspension bridge with high laminated timbers.

The uncovered Schenectady Bridge's wooden suspension truss did not work. Additional piers were built under the sagging structure, and when the bridge was eventually covered in 1825, it followed the up-and-down truss. Despite all its problems, it was not replaced until 1874.

114

In St. Lawrence County, the village of Brasher Falls had a covered bridge across the St. Regis River in the center of town.

The Brasher Falls Bridge was erected in 1863. A new bridge on Route 11 replaced the covered bridge in 1933.

This Town lattice bridge stood over Kinney's Creek at Massena Center in St. Lawrence County. It was built in 1868 by Harry F. Crooks and was replaced in 1930.

The Newfield Bridge, located just off Route 13 south of Ithaca in Tompkins County, is a bridge one can still visit. The Town lattice structure was built across the west branch of the Cayuga Inlet in 1853 for $800.

The Speedville Bridge was built across the Owego Creek by H. Seth Atkins in 1859, connecting Tompkins and Tioga Counties. It was a 60-foot-long queen-post truss that was removed in 1929.

The Halseyville Bridge in Trumansburg crossed Taughannock Creek on present Route 96 in Tompkins County. It was built by Isaac Elliott, who was assisted by Gilbert Garrett and Abram Smith.

The Halseyville Bridge was built in 1833 and was replaced in 1926. The sign on this portal advertised, "Mosher Bros. Clothiers, Trumansburg, N.Y." The sign on the other portal proclaimed, "Notice, all persons are forbidden riding or driving across this bridge faster than a walk. Penalty five dollars."

Eight

WASHINGTON COUNTY

Between Rensselaer and Washington Counties at Eagle Bridge was a big two-lane Burr arch covered bridge over the Hoosic River built in 1827. A local hunter who had shot an eagle nailed it up on the portal of the bridge. The name stayed, and an eagle was painted on the portal. The structure was replaced in 1898.

Just downstream from Eagle Bridge is Buskirk. The Buskirk Covered Bridge, between Rensselaer and Washington Counties, was built in 1857 across the Hoosic River.

The Buskirk Bridge is a 164-foot-long, single-span Howe truss bridge that one can still see. As of this writing, the bridge is closed but will undergo a complete restoration. This card is postmarked 1907.

A small bridge in Eagle Bridge was called the Carpenter's Bridge. It was a 46-foot-long Town truss across the Owlkill. When another bridge bypassed it in 1932, this bridge was abandoned. It was then removed in 1947.

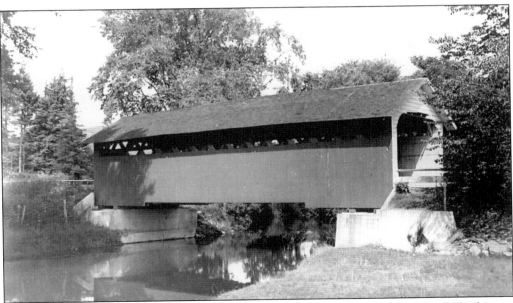

Upstream from Carpenter's Bridge stood Red, or Sheehey's, Bridge across the Owlkill. This was a 56-foot-long Town truss built in 1840. One could see the bridge just off Route 22 near Center White Creek; however, it was replaced in 1953.

Gainer's Bridge was located on Route 313 on the way from Cambridge to Arlington, Vermont. It crossed the Battenkill with a Town truss built by Caleb Orcutt in 1840. It was replaced in 1934.

Eagleville, east of Shushan, is the site for this 101-foot-long Town lattice bridge across the Battenkill. Still visible just off Route 313, the Eagleville Bridge was built by Ephraim W. Clapp in 1858.

In this photograph of the Shushan portal, advertisements are plastered on the bridge. In 1962, the bridge was bypassed by a bridge located much higher. One end of the covered bridge was moved and set on a new abutment.

This view of the Shushan Bridge shows that it had uneven spans. In 1975, after the Shushan Covered Bridge Association acquired it from the county, the bridge opened as a museum.

The Rexleigh Covered Bridge, south of Salem, is
It crosses the Battenkill with a 100-foot-long H
It is the only known covered bridge that uses th
of Troy.

OLD COVERED BRIDGE NEAR

Just down the Battenkill on Route 22, south of S
built by Caleb Orcutt in 1858 and was washed a

Battenville had a Town lattice covered bridge built in 1840 across the Battenkill. Battenville is noted for the Susan B. Anthony Home, the place where Anthony lived as a girl. Her parents are buried across the river. The covered bridge was replaced in 1916 by an iron bridge that is still in use. The tracks in the foreground are still operated by the Battenkill Railroad.

The Middle Falls Bridge was located on Route 29 near Greenwich. This view shows the falls with lots of water in the Battenkill. The bridge was replaced by a concrete arch span in 1916. This card is postmarked 1911.

In Cambridge can be found the oldest covered footbridge in the nation. The bridge was constructed in 1890 by Florans Hoxie of Easton. The bridge was built to provide access across Blair's Brook for Rice Seed Company employees and can still be seen just off Main Street in Cambridge.